Graphic Organizers That Help Struggling Students

59 Graphic Organizers Designed to Help with Time Management, Classroom Routines, Homework, Reading, and So Much More!

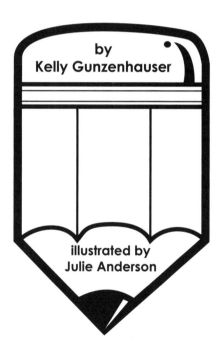

by
Kelly Gunzenhauser

illustrated by
Julie Anderson

Publisher
Key Education Publishing Company, LLC
Minneapolis, Minnesota 55438

www.keyeducationpublishing.com

CONGRATULATIONS ON YOUR PURCHASE OF A KEY EDUCATION PRODUCT!

The editors at Key Education are former teachers who bring experience, enthusiasm, and quality to each and every product. Thousands of teachers have looked to the staff at Key Education for new and innovative resources to make their work more enjoyable and rewarding. We are committed to developing educational materials that will assist teachers in building a strong and developmentally appropriate curriculum for children.

PLAN FOR GREAT TEACHING EXPERIENCES WHEN YOU USE EDUCATIONAL MATERIALS FROM KEY EDUCATION PUBLISHING COMPANY, LLC

About the Author

Kelly Gunzenhauser has a master's degree in English and taught writing at the college level. She has worked in educational publishing for 11 years and is the author of five books for teachers and children, including Key Education's *Sequencing Cut-Up Paragraphs, Creating Curriculum Using Children's Picture Books, Reading for Details,* and *Let's Learn and Play!* Kelly has two sons in preschool and spends her time playing and learning with them and volunteering at their school.

Dedication

I would like to thank the following consultants who volunteered their time and offered their expertise in order to help me write this book. I am grateful to:

- ❏ Melissa Fisch, my sounding board who always offers energy, enthusiasm, and boundless creativity.
- ❏ Pam Hill, whose curriculum information is top-notch and was most graciously given.
- ❏ Deborah Kitzman, who generously shared her time and vast expertise in dealing with students with special needs and with young students.
- ❏ Rachel Hoeing, who makes math accessible, fun, and visual, and who gave me several ideas for the math section, including the wonderful idea of "math problems around the room."

Credits

Author: Kelly Gunzenhauser
Publisher: Sherrill B. Flora
Illustrator: Julie Anderson
Editors: Karen Seberg and Claude Chalk
Cover Design and Production:
    Annette Hollister-Papp
Layout and Production: Key Education Staff

Key Education welcomes manuscripts and product ideas from teachers.
For a copy of our submission guidelines, send a self-addressed, stamped envelope to:

Key Education Publishing Company, LLC
Acquisitions Department
7309 West 112th Street
Minneapolis, Minnesota 55438

Standard Book Number: 978-1-602680-71-5
Graphic Organizers That Help Struggling Students
Copyright © 2010 by Key Education Publishing Company, LLC
Minneapolis, Minnesota 55438

Printed in the USA • All rights reserved

Contents

Introduction

It is widely known that graphic organizers enable teachers to reach out to students with different learning styles because they provide a visual basis for learning, a kinesthetic element, and a way for students to revisit prior knowledge without rereading large chunks of text. For these reasons, children who have special needs that affect their thinking and learning may benefit greatly from using graphic organizers. These children often require more than one type of instruction for retaining and recalling information. For example, when listening to instructions, a child with autism may require the additional sensory input of cutting apart information and physically arranging it in order. A child with ADHD may better comprehend reading if he can take breaks to write or draw about it. A child with an auditory difficulty will benefit if information is offered in a visual format as well as verbally. A child with dyslexia may recall information better if she can look back at a summary she wrote instead of rereading a chapter. Students with special needs often require extra practice when learning new skills, which is provided though the use of graphic organizers.

The graphic organizers in this book are designed to provide additional learning reinforcement for students of all abilities and learning styles, including students with special needs. The features in this book that target students with special needs include:

- Spatial and visual modifications such as darker, heavier cutting lines; larger spaces in which to do work; and simple directions in easy-to-read print.
- Multiple steps that are easy to cut apart or obscure when copying so that work can be introduced in shorter chunks.
- Flexible directions that allow children to either draw or write. (In many cases, the teacher will supply the directions entirely.)

When working with a graphic organizer, it is important to remember that the point is mastering the information or the skill being taught and not mastering the organizer itself. Graphic organizers are useful when they help children categorize, retain, and recall information. However, learning to independently fill out certain organizers is beneficial; if students have used a particular organizer before, they can usually apply their experience to help them use it with other information. Used effectively for these two purposes, a graphic organizer becomes an effective scaffold for reviewing previously learned information and learning new information.

Included in this resource are organizers to help with time management and scheduling, classroom routines, socialization, reading, writing, mathematics, science, and social studies. Look at the beginning of each section for instructions for how to use each organizer, as well as suggestions for creating your own class-specific organizers or modifying the ones you already have.

Most importantly, remember that using an organizer can be a fun "break" for students, even as they continue learning. Using organizers gives them a chance to be creative, draw and write more freely, and take more ownership over their learning. If you enjoy your class time with graphic organizers and look forward to them as a special treat, chances are your students will, too.

Tips for Using General Classroom Organizers

Students often benefit from knowing what is coming next, from getting a prompt about what to do in certain situations, or from help with planning and evaluating. These organizers familiarize students with routines, procedures, and life skills.

Calendar Grid and Daily Schedule

Use the Calendar Grid (page 8) and Daily Schedule (page 9) organizers to remind students what is coming next. Students can label and number the organizers, or you can pre-label one and make multiple copies. To save paper, laminate the organizers and let students label them with washable markers; then, hang the organizers from their desks to prevent smudging.

Cutout Symbols for the Calendar Grid and Daily Schedule

Copy the Cutout Symbols (page 10) on card stock for use with the Calendar Grid and Daily Schedule. Students can attach the pieces with adhesive putty or hook-and-loop dots. For the Daily Schedule, you may choose to let students remove each symbol as it passes so that they can keep track of where they are in their day and know when it is time to go home.

Start-to-Finish

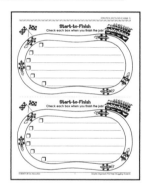

Program the Start-to-Finish organizer (page 11) to show students what to expect at the beginning of the day, the end of the day, or for each lesson. For example, before copying the organizer, write everything you want students to do at the beginning of the day (put away backpacks, sharpen pencils, take out paper, etc.) or the end of the day (gather homework together, put on jackets, etc.) and have them check off each task when it is completed. You can also use this page to help students learn how you prefer to structure lessons. For example, if you usually collect homework first, write that in the first blank. Add other things you do consistently in all lessons, such as return homework, review yesterday's lesson, learn something new, provide practice for what you learned, and assign new homework. This form can help you make your agenda more consistent for those students who crave predictability.

Computer Procedures

Most classrooms now have computers or at least have scheduled computer time. Teach students to be as autonomous as possible by writing down your steps for computer use on the Computer Procedures organizer (page 12). If students need to turn on the computers, list that first. If they have to keep track of their own time, prompt them to check the clock. Use the spaces to remind students of assignments and simply cover the extra spaces with white paper before copying.

All About Me

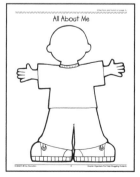

Students can create informative portraits with the All About Me organizer (page 13). Have them color copies of it to resemble themselves, their classmates (in getting-to-know-you exercises), or family members, or to represent book characters or historical figures. To gather specific information, write a label outside each body part and let students write inside each body part. For example, label the head with name, the torso with birthday, the arms with my family and my friends, and the legs with I like and I dislike. Or, if you are studying a historical figure, label the head with name, the torso with birthday, and the arms with accomplishments. For an extra challenge, let students cut out the body parts, reassemble them by gluing them to another piece of paper, and rewrite the labels.

Today I Feel . . .

Often, a student will come to class in a bad mood and you have no idea why—and she may not know either. Young students, especially those with special needs, may have trouble communicating their feelings. Crack the code with the Today, I Feel . . . organizer (page 14) Students should cut out the "window" and frame the picture that tells how they feel. Let students write the reasons behind their feelings on the lines under the grid or simply cover the lines with paper before copying. You can also use this as a simple writing prompt by having each student write an imaginary event on the lines and then use the frame to show how she would feel if that event happened.

What is the Problem?

Problem-solving skills can be difficult to teach. Use the versatile What's the Problem? organizer (page 15) to help students identify and resolve problems. If students want to attempt multiple solutions, cut off the "Did Your Idea Work?" portion and make additional copies of it for students to write about whether the problem has been solved each time. This can be a helpful tool to assist students in resolving classroom conflicts or problems they are having with their own behavior or study habits. Students can also use this organizer to identify problems and predict solutions for math story problems, to predict plot resolutions in stories, and to predict outcomes in science experiments and historical events.

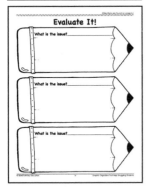

Evaluate It!

Asking students their opinions empowers them to think critically about likes, dislikes, issues, and the solutions to those issues. Let students fill out an Evaluate It! organizer (page 16) any time you want their opinions. Fill in the first line with what you want them to evaluate: classroom rules and procedures, school in general, a friendship, the current seating chart, cafeteria food, a recently read story, a math lesson, a holiday custom, things about their home state, school in general, a field trip, bad weather policies, etc. On the following lines the students can write down their opinions.

Be a Good _____! Picture Chart

There will be times when you need students to think about what it takes to be good at something, or to prepare them for an upcoming situation. The Be a Good _____! picture chart (page 17) helps students list aspects of excellence. Use this organizer to prepare students for events or to help them find strengths and weaknesses in themselves, in others, in characters, or in historical figures. Fill in the blank with any word you like that is relevant: friend, listener, classmate, teacher (if you want their feedback), student, audience, guest, sport, visitor, writer, reader, mathematician, inventor, scientist, athlete, test taker, artist, musician, etc. If you prefer for students to write, have them write words in the boxes rather than draw. Cut off the bottom portion of the page if you wish to make the assignment shorter.

Climb to Your Goal Organizer

Letting students set their own goals and plan how to reach them gives students ownership over their success. The Climb to Your Goal organizer (page 18) helps individual students set personal goals and outline strategies for achieving them. You can enlarge the organizer and post it to set class project goals such as fund-raisers; improving grades or test scores; increasing physical fitness; memorizing spelling, vocabulary words, or math facts; or completing science fair projects. Students can also use this organizer to map out how goals were achieved by others.

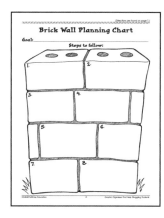

Brick Wall Planning Chart

Sometimes students are overwhelmed by writing down chronological steps for a project. It may help them to simply think of everything they need to do first and then put the steps in order later. The Brick Wall Planning Chart (page 19) helps students get the steps on paper; then afterwards, students organize the steps so that they don't have to do both at once. Begin by having the students write each thing they need to do, one thing per brick; next, let them cut apart the bricks and arrange them in order on another sheet of paper. They can then tape the bricks to their paper. If you provide laminated paper on which to tape the bricks, each student can easily rearrange them or add more even after taping. This is a good organizer to use with any multitask project such as putting on a performance, creating complex artwork, solving math word problems, completing science or social studies projects, writing research papers, or doing other group projects.

Recipe for Success

The Recipe for Success organizer (page 20) can be used on its own or after students use the Climb to Your Goal Organizer or Brick Wall Planning Chart. Once students figure out their steps and materials, they can write them on the recipe cards in a more orderly fashion. Use this as a study guide, for project planning, or for any other goal-setting exercise. Students can also write regular recipes on the cards, of course.

The Homework Checklist

The Homework Checklist (page 21) is aimed at helping those students who have a hard time keeping take-home work organized. Let them keep copies of the checklist at their desks. Each morning, announce that it is time for students to get out new Homework Checklists and tape them to their desks. As you assign homework throughout the day, allot time for students to write down their homework assignments, materials, and due dates. (Make sure students transfer their long-term assignments from one checklist to the next, and help them break the assignments into smaller parts to stay on track.) At the end of the day, have students untape their checklists and take them home. Students can use the "Bring Back" blanks to help them repack their backpacks. Collect the organizers with the homework each morning as students are getting out new ones. You might consider having students maintain special homework take-home folders and collecting all of the homework at once when possible, to cut down on time spent shuffling papers.

Secret Message

Students will love using this organizer. Many students, particularly those with special needs, will hesitate to ask questions about assignments because they are afraid of not looking smart. Students may also have insights to share with their teachers but are uncomfortable offering feedback. Draw this hidden information from students with the Secret Message organizer (page 21). Cut a slit in the lid of a box and place it near your desk. Designate times for all students to write comments or questions on the copies of the organizer, explaining that students do not have to sign their names. Some good times for using the organizer include a few days before taking a difficult test, assignment, or project; if any students seem lost or out of sorts; if students seem to be arguing; or even regularly such as once a week. You can direct students' comments or leave them open-ended. After you collect questions and comments, decide when and how you want to read and respond to them. You may wish to read the comments while students are doing seat work and then choose to respond to some in the class setting and some individually.

Month:

Sunday	Monday	Tuesday	Wednesday	Thursday	Friday	Saturday

Today is _____ Date _____

Time	Activity

Time	Activity

(Directions are found on page 5.)

Cutout Symbols for Calendar Grid and Daily Schedule Organizers

Reading	Math	Spelling	Writing
Science	Social Studies	Physical Education	Music
Lunch	Snack	Recess	Computer
Media Center	Art	Visitor	Field Trip
Wash Hands	Bathroom	Time to go home	

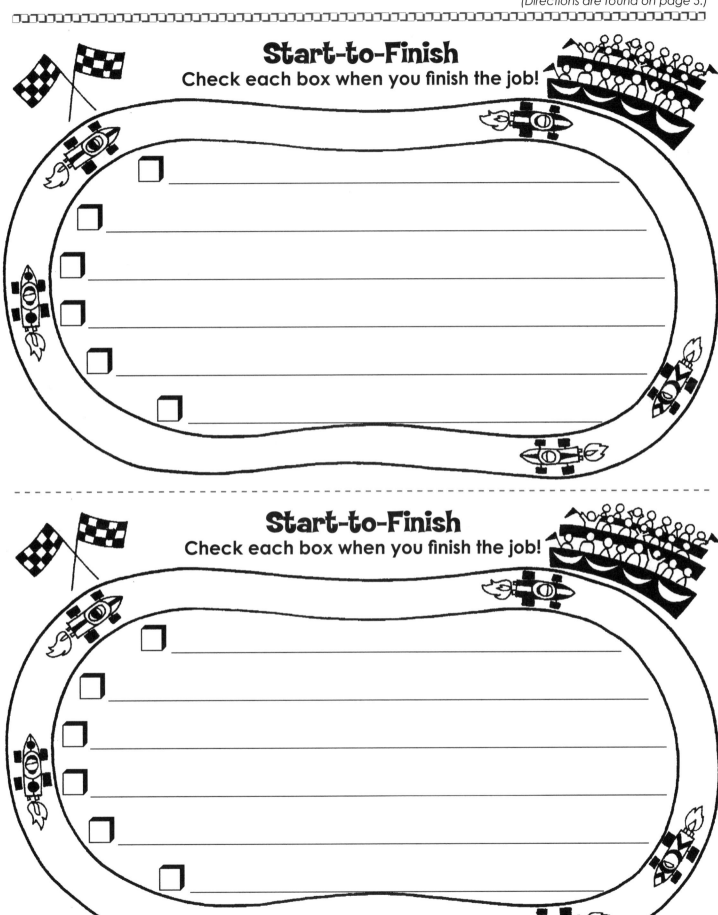

Start-to-Finish
Check each box when you finish the job!

Start-to-Finish
Check each box when you finish the job!

COMPUTER PROCEDURES

1._____

2._____

3._____

4._____

5._____

6._____

All About Me

Today, I Feel . . .

Happy

Sad

Sleepy

Hungry

Angry

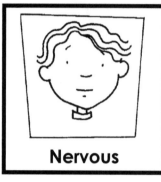

Nervous

Afraid

Excited

Silly

Sick

Bored

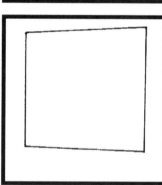

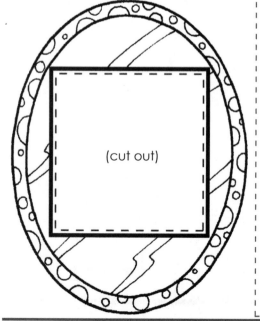

(cut out)

Here's why: _____

_____

_____

_____

_____

_____

(Directions are found on page 6.)

What is the problem? ______________________________

____

____

Why is it a problem? ______________________________

____

____

How can the problem be solved?

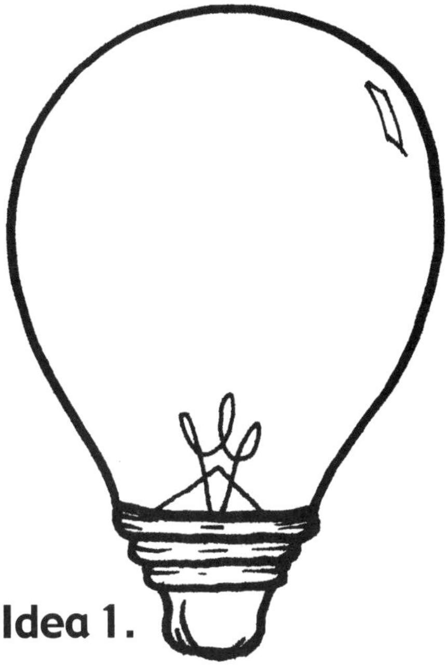

Idea 1.

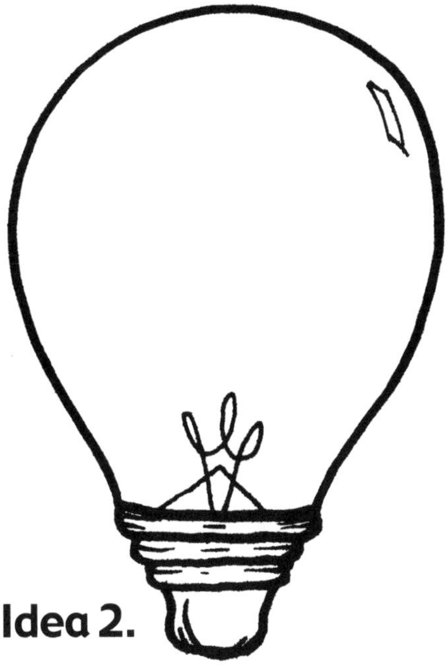

Idea 2.

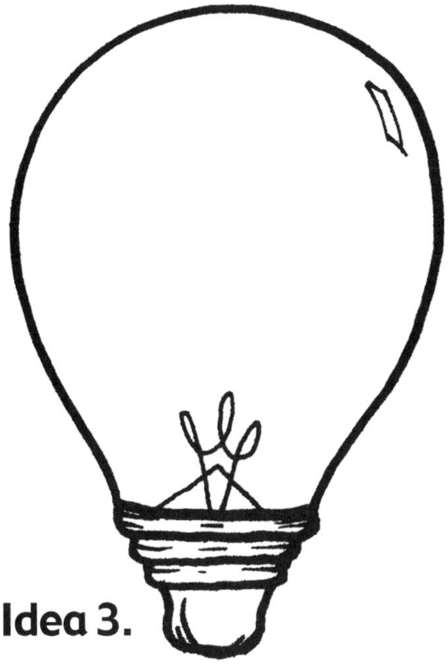

Idea 3.

Write #1 under the idea you want to try first.

Did your idea work? ______________________________

Why or why not? ______________________________

____

Evaluate It!

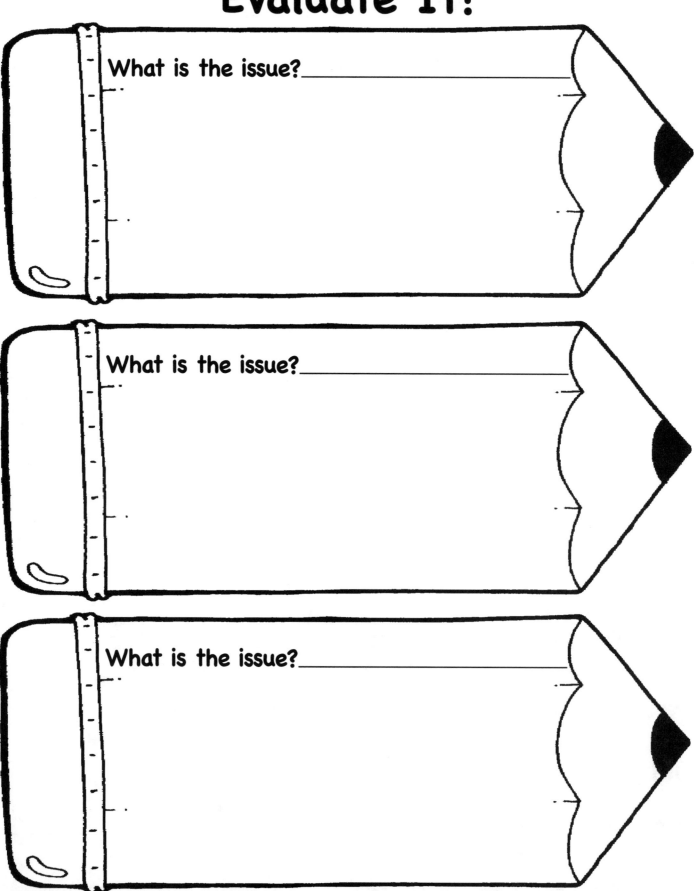

What is the issue?_____

What is the issue?_____

What is the issue?_____

Be a Good _____!

1. _____

2. _____

3. _____

4. _____

Climb to Your Goal!

Goal: _____

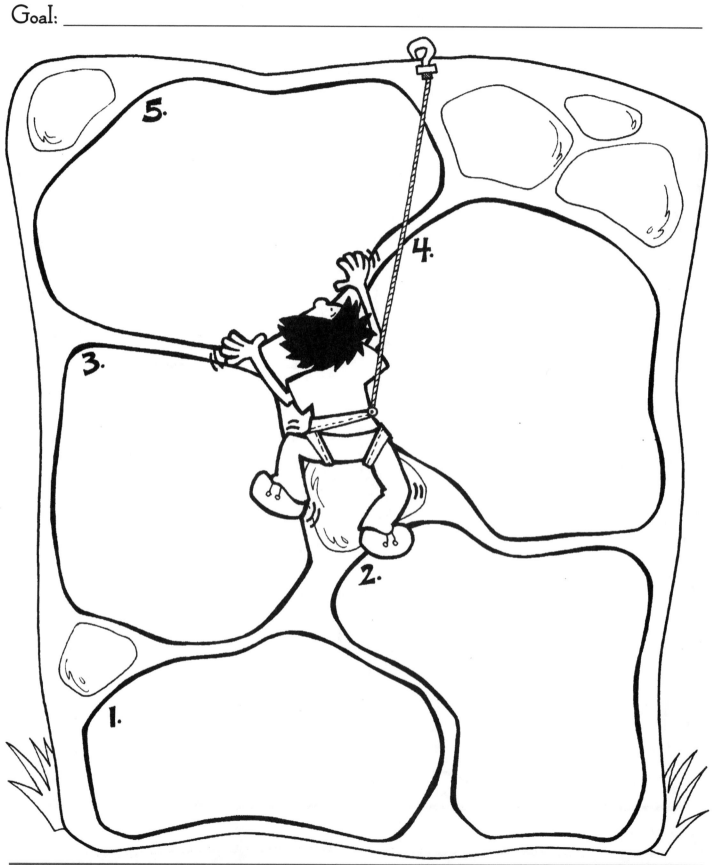

(Directions are found on page 7.)

Brick Wall Planning Chart

Goal:_____

Steps to follow:

1.

2.

3.

4.

5.

6.

7.

8.

Recipe for Success

Project Theme: _____

Things I need: _____

_____

_____

_____

_____

Notes: _____

_____

_____

_____

_____

Step 1: _____

Step 2: _____

Step 3: _____

Step 4: _____

Step 5: _____

Step 6: _____

Step 7: _____

Step 8: _____

Graphic Organizers

KE-804076 © Key Education

The Homework Checklist

Assignment	Take Home	Bring Back
1.	1.	1.
2.	2.	2.
3.	3.	3.
4.	4.	4.

Child's Signature: _____

Parent's Signature: _____

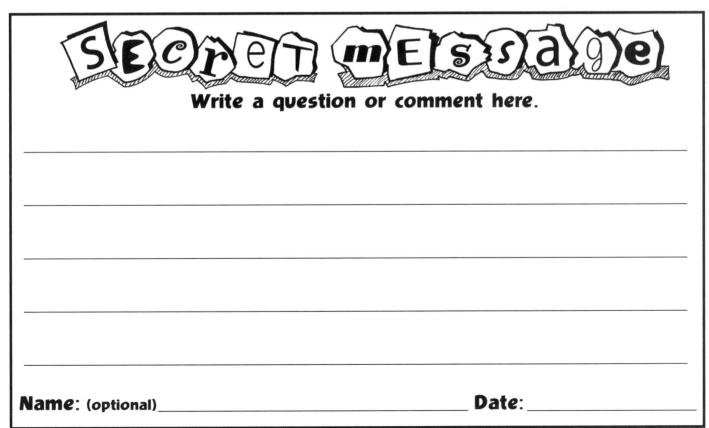

Secret Message

Write a question or comment here.

_____

_____

_____

_____

_____

Name: (optional) _____ **Date**: _____

Tips for Using General Academic Organizers

These organizers can help students complete many general academic tasks in all subject areas, such as comprehending what they read, sorting and organizing information, finding main ideas, understanding the progression of events, and generating ideas. Included with the organizers are ideas for using them across the curriculum.

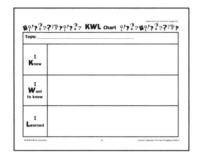

KWL Chart

The KWL chart (page 24) is one of the most popular graphic organizers for elementary school. Traditionally, it is used to let students think about what they **Know** about a topic and what they **Want to Know** as they embark on learning about the topic and then to recap **What They Learned**. Use this when students are learning about any new topic. For example, if you are teaching a new book in class, students can talk about what they think they know from looking at the book or what they know about the author. They can use the KWL Chart as a brainstorming tool for any writing assignment or subject-area reading assignment. In math, students can use this chart to dissect the steps of a story problem or assess their current understanding of geometry, fractions, measurement, or even math facts.

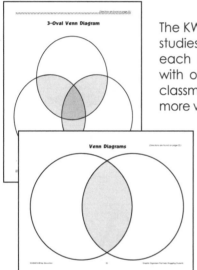

The KWL chart is an obvious organizer to use with acquiring new scientific or social studies knowledge. It can also be fun to use when students are first getting to know each other. Children who have difficulty making friends may find connecting with others less abstract if they can classify information they learn about their classmates. This version of the KWL chart is organized horizontally to allow students more writing space, but students can also draw pictures in the space if they prefer.

Venn Diagram

Good old Venn diagrams (pages 25 and 26) are still one of the best visual ways to compare and contrast. There are two Venn Diagrams in this book. One is a two-circle Venn, and the other is a three-oval Venn. Use the diagrams to compare book characters, stories, animals, plants, planets, holidays, customs, and even student characteristics. For example, if you are comparing two animals, such as a bat and a bird, have students write things they have in common (they both fly, they each have two legs, etc.) in the intersecting space, and things that are different (birds have feathers, bats have fur, etc.) in the outer spaces.

Sorting Buckets

Sorting is an important skill. Use the Sorting Buckets organizer (page 27) to help students sort objects by size, color, or other properties; sort animals or foods into categories; sort holiday symbols; sort months into seasons; and sort word families, numbers, and more. The buckets are large enough for students to use the organizer for three-dimensional objects, but they can also write words or draw pictures inside them. You can write categories underneath the buckets or let students work it out on their own. You can also cover one or two buckets with white paper before copying to reduce the number of categories.

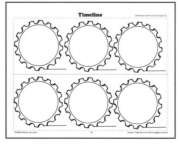

Timeline

The Timeline organizer (page 28) can help students fill in story events, relay historic events, track steps for science experiments, and even flesh out problems that arise in class or around the school as they work out how to solve them. Single-page timelines can frustrate students because of too little writing space, so copy the page several times and let students tape them together so that they have plenty of room to write or draw.

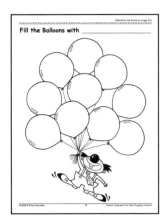

Fill the Balloons with _____

The Fill the Balloons organizer (page 29) is one of the most flexible organizers. It serves the same purpose as a web, but because there is a finite number of blanks to fill, it is much more manageable for students. In the blank provided, write guidelines for what students should use to "fill" the balloons: math facts for a certain number, words that describe a book character, word family words, writing ideas, characteristics of a certain animal, traits of being a good citizen, etc. If there are more balloons than needed, for example, addition facts for 5, let students color the remaining balloons.

Brainstorm List

One major complaint teachers have with allowing students to create brainstorming webs is that they are messy and overwhelming. Students with special needs can find creating the web—the graphic part of this exercise—more challenging than generating the material for the actual list. The Brainstorm List (page 30) is a simple graphic organizer that lets students focus on content. Use this organizer as you would any brainstorming web for writing; for making predictions; to list character traits, math facts, or events in sequence; for scientific categorizing, or even as a homework reminder. Shorten the list spaces or provide a place for drawing by covering the lines with white paper before copying. To help students narrow their lists, let them use highlighters to choose the most relevant items.

The Bookmaker

The Bookmaker (page 30) is a very basic organizer that allows for many possibilities. For example, if students are learning about a new holiday, they can draw some of the symbols for that holiday and then explain them on the writing lines. They can staple multiple pages together to write and illustrate picture books, math facts with corresponding sets, alphabet books, vocabulary books, science books, history books, biographies, newspaper articles, etc. You can also supply the picture and instruct students to write to a picture prompt. Have students use the first writing line to caption the drawing or photo, and the organizer title is de-emphasized so that students can supply their own titles. Finally, a unique way to use this as a math story problem organizer is to let each student write his own story problem on the paper and draw a picture representation of the problem without solving it. Post all of the unsolved problems around the room, and let each student number a sheet of paper, walk around the room, and write her answers to the problems.

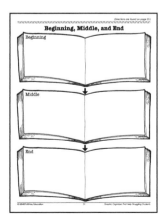

Beginning, Middle, and End Organizer

Although Beginning, Middle, and End organizers (page 31) are usually for retelling stories, students can use this organizer for chapter books or textbook summaries, organizing the parts of science experiments, retelling biographies, recalling events, and even math story problems. This organizer gives students the option of illustrating as well as writing.

KWL Chart

Topic: _____

I **K**now	I **W**ant to know	I **L**earned

KE-804076 © Key Education

Graphic Organizers

2-Circle Venn Diagram

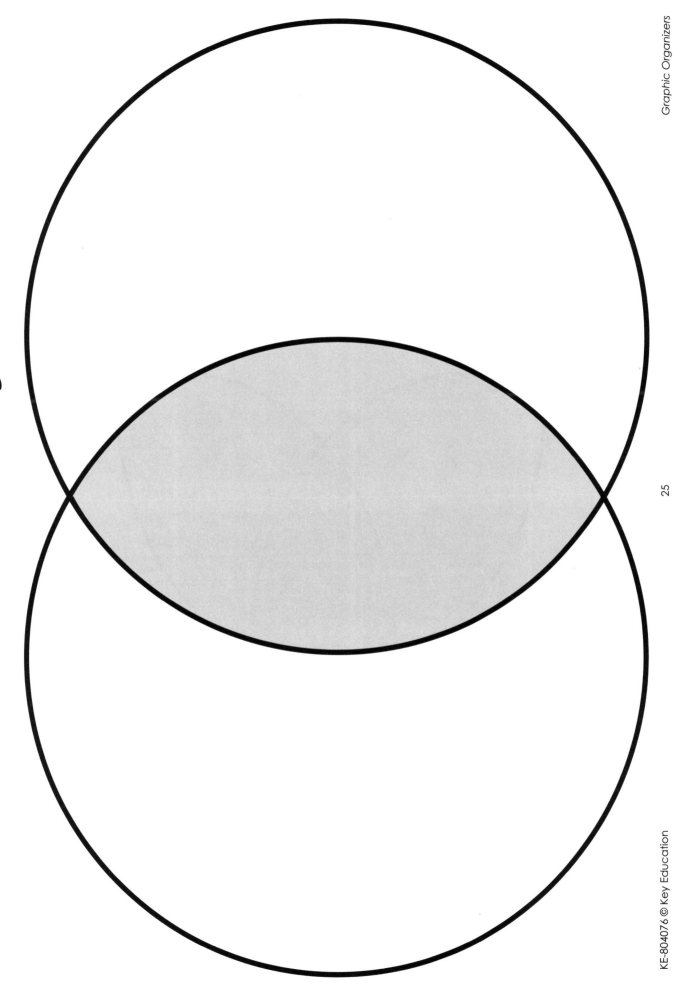

3-Oval Venn Diagram

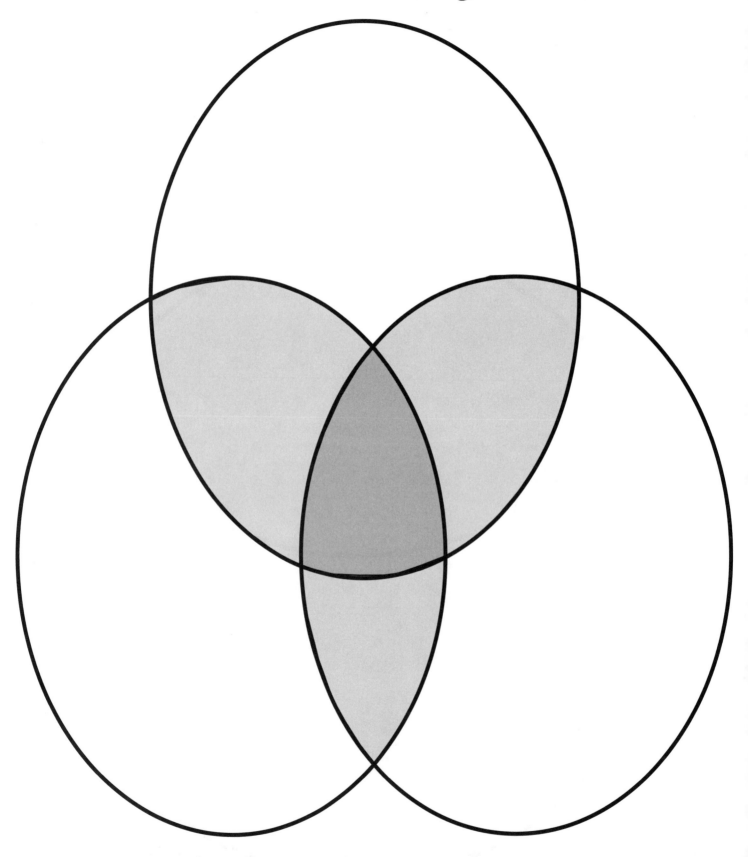

sorting Buckets
Sort into the four buckets.

Graphic Organizers

Timeline

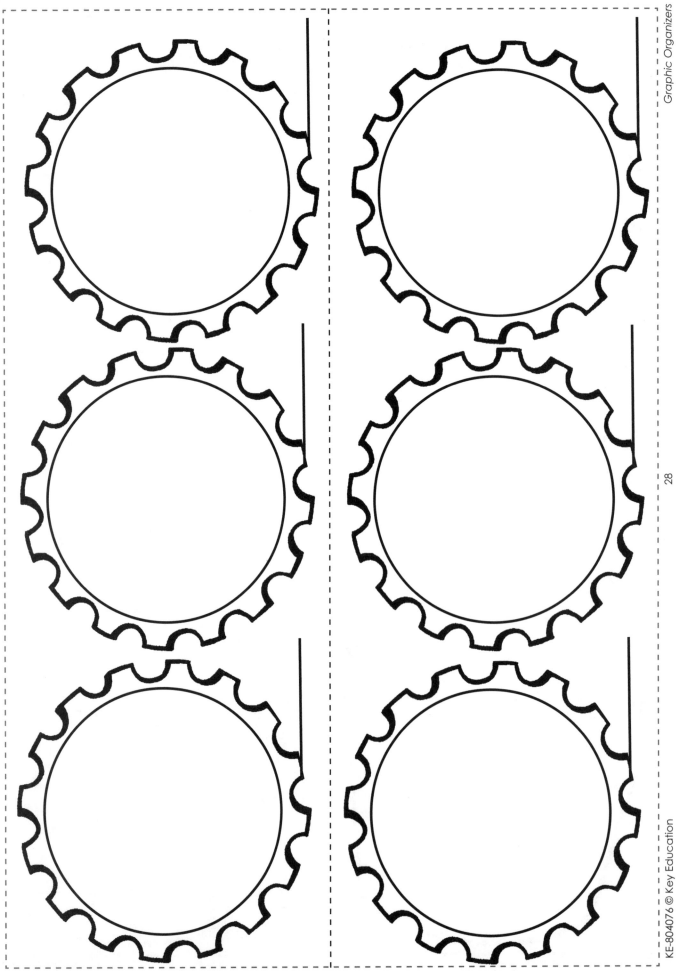

Fill the Balloons with _____

(Directions are found on page 23.)

Brainstorm List

List: _____

_____

_____

_____

_____

_____

_____

_____

_____

_____

_____

_____

_____

Title

The Bookmaker

_____

_____

_____

_____

_____

_____

_____

_____

_____

_____

_____

_____

_____

(Directions are found on page 23.)

Beginning, Middle, and End

Beginning

Middle

End

Tips for Using Reading and Writing Organizers

These organizers help students retain information gathered from reading and also help make writing less overwhelming. Ample writing and drawing space is provided so that students can use the organizers easily to record all of their ideas.

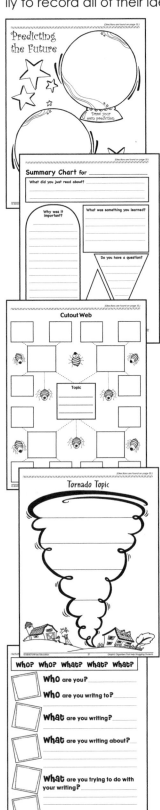

Predicting the Future

Predicting the Future (page 34) covers the picture walk exercise many teachers like to do. Let students take a picture walk and illustrate something they think will happen in the book. Then, after reading, have them draw something related to the prediction that actually did happen. You can also guide the exercise by writing a question, such as, What do you think the smallest animal in *The Napping House* will be? Of course, this organizer can also be used to make predictions for social studies and science experiments.

Summary Chart

Students who have difficulty reading and retaining information will find taking breaks to write, draw, and summarize their reading helpful. They should turn to the Summary Chart (page 35) periodically during their reading to write or draw their recollections. To use the chart as a study aid, let students highlight their notes as they reread them, using different colors to categorize the information, if possible. They can also use this organizer to recap information from talks and lectures.

Cutout Web

Information that students put into a brainstorming web often does not actually end up in their writing. Webbing can seem like a separate, disconnected activity rather than prewriting. Students should brainstorm ideas or events in the Cutout Web (page 36) as they would in a web of their own design. After students write, ask them to look in their writing for each detail from the web, cut out the square when they find it in their writing, and tape it to a separate sheet of construction paper. Have them turn in their writing, their taped cutout pages, and the remainders of the webs, and you will be able to see exactly what details they used (or thought they used) and what they left behind. They can also use the taped pages to self-check that they have included enough details if you require them to include a certain amount of squares from their webs in their writing.

The Tornado Topic

Some students have a tendency to choose very broad writing topics for reports, like "dogs" or "space." The Tornado Topic organizer (page 37) helps them narrow their topics. Model the organizer by putting a copy on the overhead. Note that it is shaped like a tornado. Explain that a tornado comes from very big clouds overhead, but the bottom of a tornado is much smaller and more precise. On the overhead, write a very broad topic on the line provided. For example, you could write "Dogs." In the next space, write a narrowed topic, like "My dog." Continue by writing "My dog likes to dig." In the bottom space, write "My dog dug up a snake and ate it." Ask if students would be more interested in reading about this topic than about the topic "Dogs." Then, distribute the organizer and let students try to narrow their topics.

Who? Who? What? What? What?

For many student writers, the writer is always "me" and the audience is always "the teacher," and the purpose is always "because she told me to write something." Use the Who? Who? What? What? What? organizer (page 38) to help students break out of their usual identities for some creative writing. Let students fill in their own blanks, fill them in for each other, or you can fill them in.

Writing Planner

Getting started writing is hard for some students. The Writing Planner organizer (page 39) leads students through writing a paragraph. After they answer the questions, guide students through rewriting their answers to make paragraphs. Eventually, students will internalize the process and be able to write better paragraphs without the organizer.

Friendly Letter

The Friendly Letter template (page 40) shows students the format for writing a letter. Since the writing lines are shorter than most templates, you can copy the letter on decorative computer stationery or let students decorate their own edges.

Word Bank

Encourage students to "invest" in new words with the Word Bank organizer (page 41). Write down words you would like students to use in the "coins" or encourage them to add their own vocabulary words to the coins. Have students cut out the coins; then, each time they use one of the targeted words, let them tape that coin to the piggy bank. To deter students from using tired words (*nice, happy, pretty,* etc.), add those words to the bottom of the page. Add a coin for each target word used, but each time you find one of the listed words in a student's work, have him remove a coin from the piggy bank. Be sure to give the student the opportunity to replace the tired words so that he can get his coins back into the bank.

Editing Treasure Hunt

Put a positive spin on proofing with the Editing Treasure Hunt organizer (page 42). Students can either proof their own papers or swap with another student. On the treasure chest, write the particular errors you want students to search for: capitalization errors, missing punctuation, misspelled words, overused words, etc. As each mistake is found, students may mark the correction on the paper, and then they can color in a gold doubloon. You can also use this organizer to have students unscramble words or to find math facts that match an answer.

Editing Checklist

Most classrooms have an Editing Checklist (page 43). Hopefully, you will find that this one is more visual and therefore easier for the children to use than most of the other editing checklists. Distribute this list to students and let them check their own writing. Record your own additional items on the blank lines at the bottom of the organizer.

(Directions are found on page 32.)

Predicting the Future

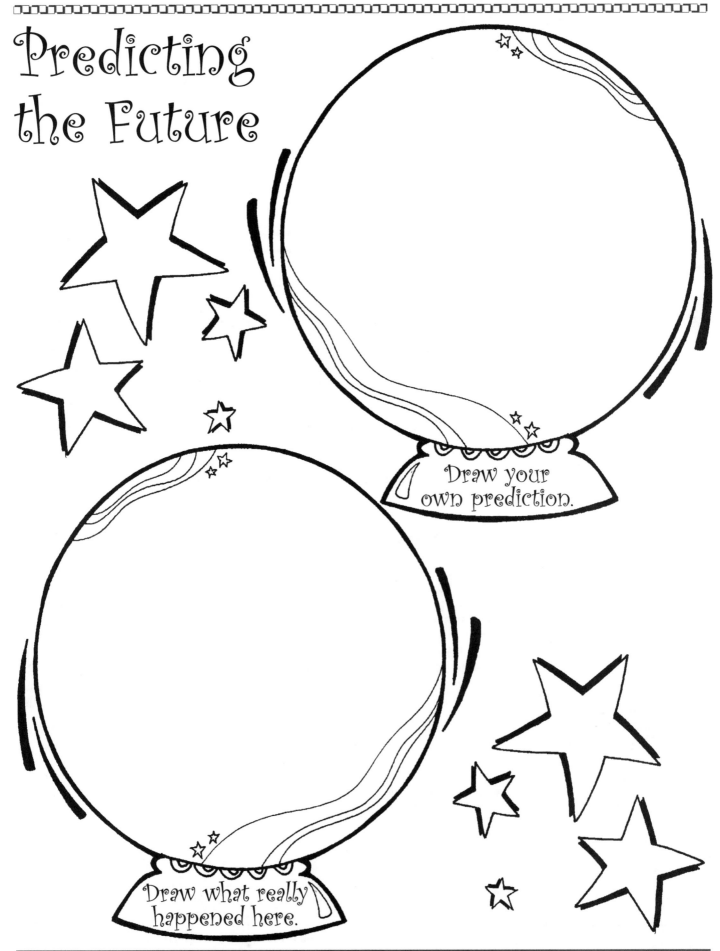

Draw your own prediction.

Draw what really happened here.

(Directions are found on page 32.)

Summary Chart for ______________________

What did you just read about? ______________________

____

____

Why was it important?

____

What was something you learned?

____

Do you have a question?

____

Draw something from what you read.

(Directions are found on page 32.)

Cutout Web

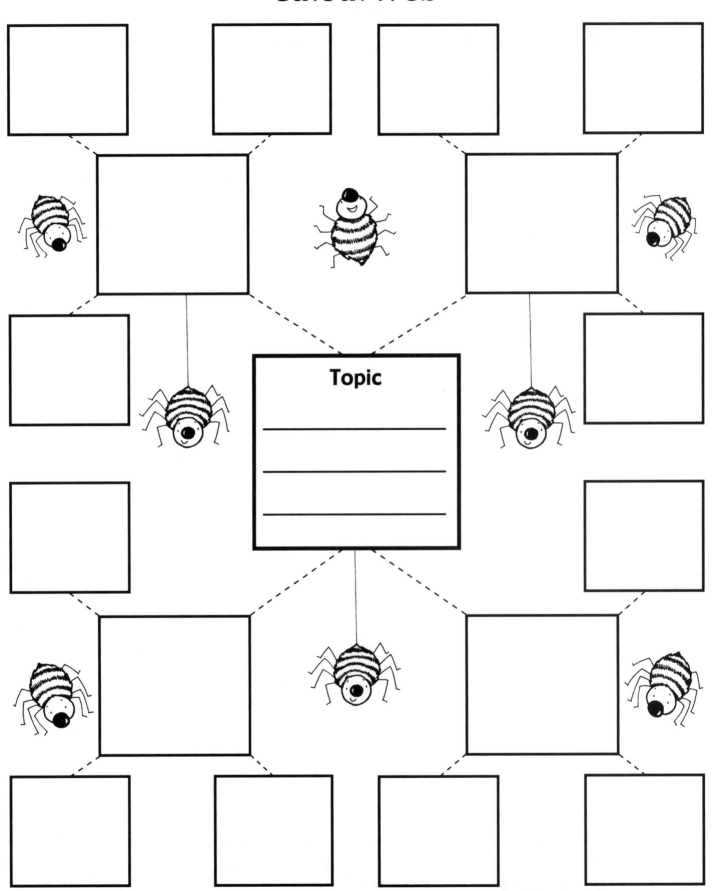

Topic

Tornado Topic

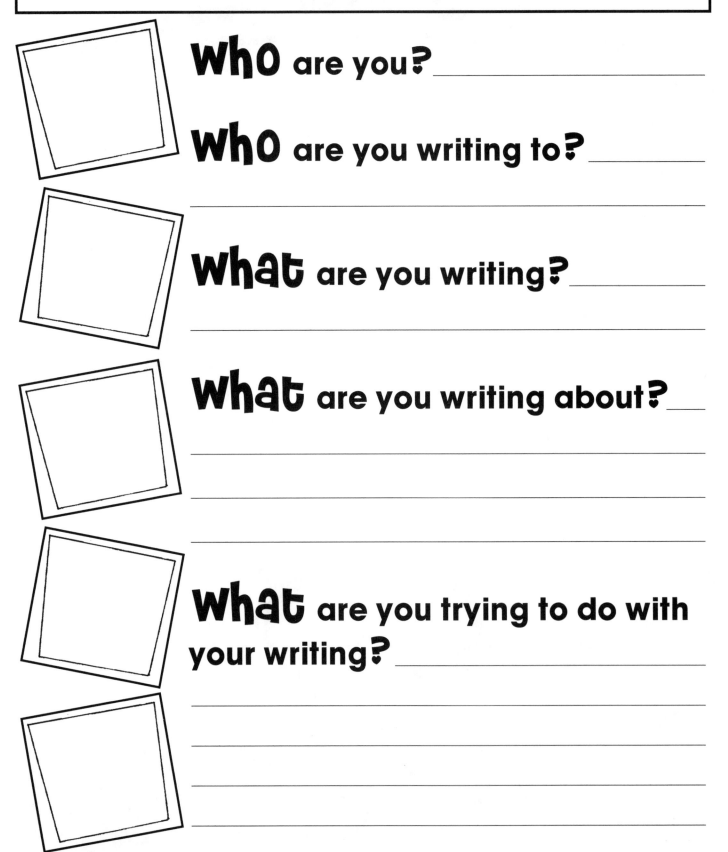

who? who? what? what? what?

who are you? _____

who are you writing to? _____

_____

what are you writing? _____

_____

what are you writing about? ____

_____

_____

what are you trying to do with your writing? _____

_____

_____

_____

(Directions are found on page 33.)

Writing Planner

What are you writing about? ______________________________

____

____

Who are you writing for, besides your teacher? ______________________________

____

____

List or draw 3 details you want to include:

1.

2.

3.

What is your first sentence going to say? ______________________________

____

____

How do you want your writing to end? ______________________________

____

____

(Directions are found on page 33.)

FRIENDLY LETTER

Dear ______________________________,

______________________________,

____
signature

Word Bank

Editing Treasure Hunt

(Directions are found on page 33.)

Editing Checklist

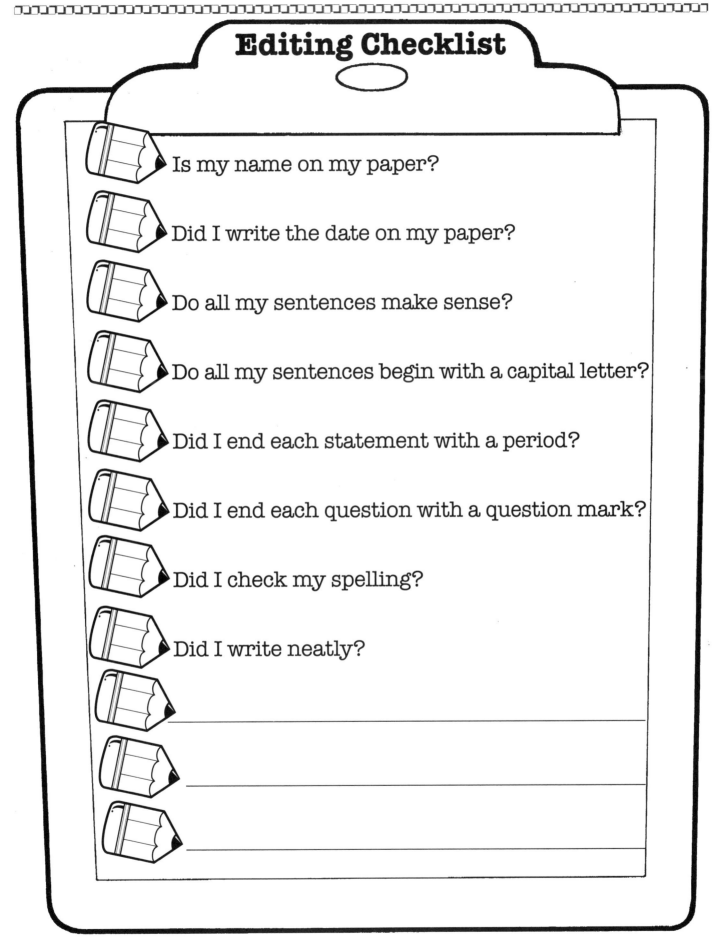

Is my name on my paper?

Did I write the date on my paper?

Do all my sentences make sense?

Do all my sentences begin with a capital letter?

Did I end each statement with a period?

Did I end each question with a question mark?

Did I check my spelling?

Did I write neatly?

_____

_____

_____

Tips for Using Math Graphic Organizers

Math graphic organizers are effective because they give concrete representations of concepts that are sometimes abstract or hard to picture: computations, shapes, measurements, etc. Children who have a hard time with mental computations will especially benefit from using these graphic organizers.

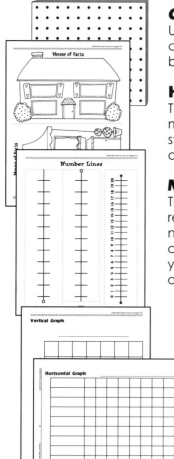

Geoboard
Use this print version of a Geoboard (page 45) to reinforce shapes. Students can connect the dots to make any shape. Add a three-dimensional element by letting students trace blocks or match blocks to pretraced shapes.

House of Facts
The House of Facts (page 46) is a version of a basic teaching tool that makes math fact families more visual. Write the fact numbers on the roof and let students fill in the windows and door with the corresponding problems. Two different house have been provided.

Number Lines
The Number Lines (page 47) are blank except for one so that students will realize that the numbers get larger as they go left to right. Be creative with the number lines. Let students use a highlighter to color specific numbers for skip counting, or use it to complete math problems. Reproduce as many sections as your students may need. Let the children keep the numbered versions at their desks for reference.

Horizontal and Vertical Graphs
Use the Horizontal and Vertical Graphs (pages 48-49) to help children create picture graphs, line graphs, and bar graphs—perhaps the easiest way to help them gather and represent data. Let children make the graphs by adding objects to create vertical or horizontal bars, coloring spaces in the grid to create bar graphs, or by plotting points and drawing lines. Examples could be:
- ❏ **Pictographs/bar graphs:** pet ownership; personal characteristics and preferences such as eye color, shirt color, favorite ice cream flavor; tracking events such as item sales or weather occurrences.
- ❏ **Line graphs:** things that rise and fall such as daily high temperatures, or number of classmates who bring their lunch, or who were out sick.

Measure Minder
The Measure Minder (page 50) is like a cheat sheet to help students remember what tools measure which properties. This organizer also familiarizes students with the terminology for units of measurement appropriate to each tool or set of tools. Focus on either metric or standard measures by covering the terms you do not want to teach.

Just the Facts (Addition and Subtraction)
Math fact practice is important for students, but it can be dull work. Make it more interesting with the programmable Just the Facts organizers (pages 51–52). Each page has an arrow and target illustration at the top. Write the target number in the circle in the middle of the target, then let students fill in the blank addition or subtraction spaces with fact families. You can also program the organizers yourself to make a more traditional worksheet, or let student pairs work together to create worksheets. Simplify the organizer by cutting off the bottom of the sheet, or by covering one or more rows before copying. If you want to mix addition and subtraction on the same sheet, draw vertical lines through some of the minus signs on the subtraction organizer.

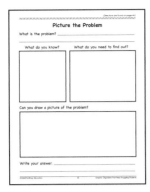

Picture the Problem

For some students, math problems are difficult to solve without a concrete representation. If you are working on word problems or problems that students could solve by using counters or pictures, let students work them out on the Picture the Problem (page 53) graphic organizer. Students have ample space to write the problem, draw it, do calculations, and then explain why they solved it, which is an important step that can lead to greater understanding of similar problems. Rewriting the problem with the answer at the bottom helps each student restate his solution.

Geoboard

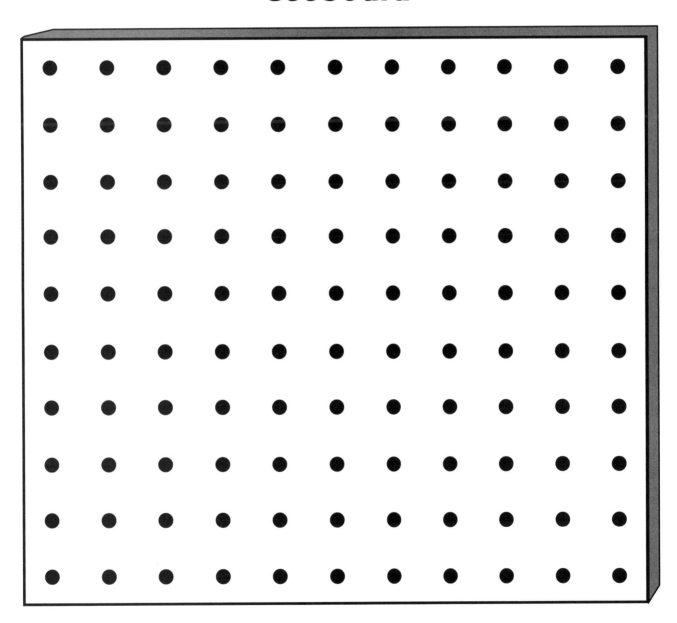

House of Facts

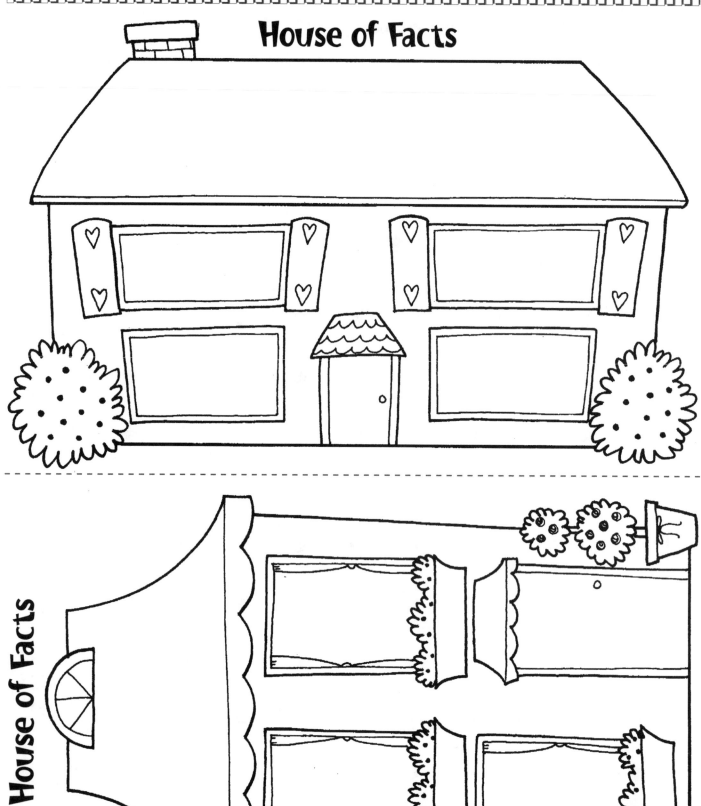

House of Facts

Number Lines

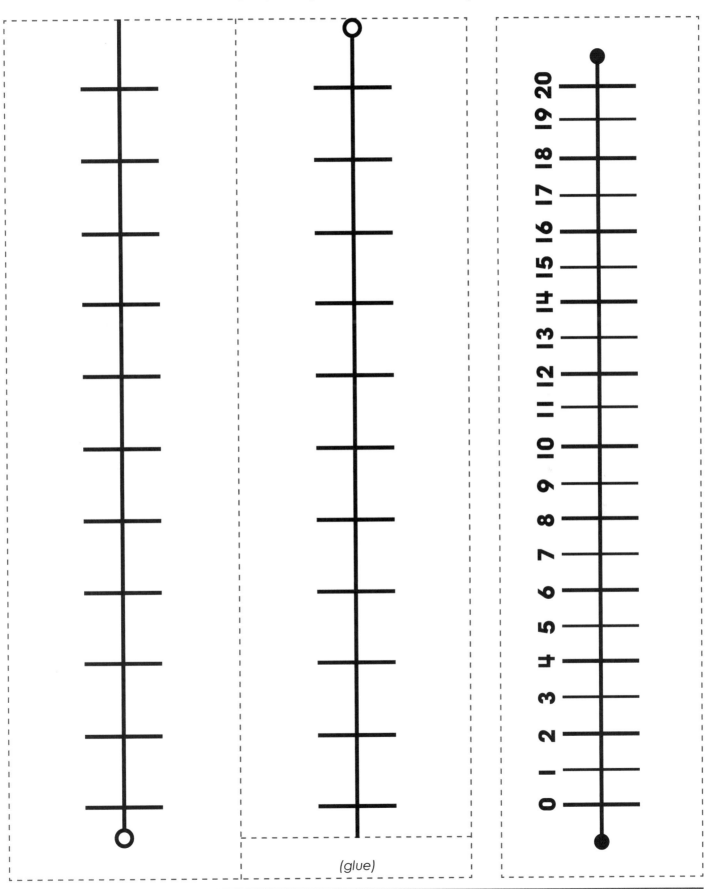

(glue)

Horizontal Graph

(Directions are found on page 44.)

Vertical Graph

Measure Minder

Volume

cups, teaspoons, ounces

milliliters, liters

Weight & Mass

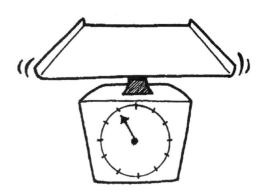

pounds, ounces

milligrams, grams, decigrams

Length, Height, Area

inches, feet, yards, miles

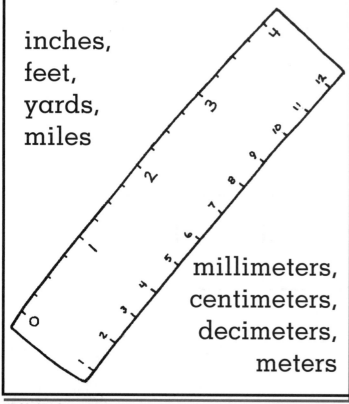

millimeters, centimeters, decimeters, meters

Time

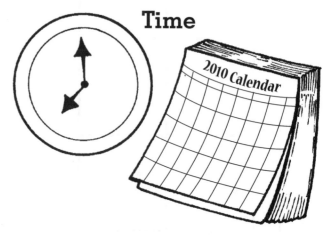

seconds, minutes, hours

days, weeks, months, years

Just the Facts - Addition

_____ + _____ = _____   _____ + _____ = _____

_____ + _____ = _____   _____ + _____ = _____

_____ + _____ = _____   _____ + _____ = _____

_____ + _____ = _____   _____ + _____ = _____

_____ + _____ = _____   _____ + _____ = _____

_____ + _____ = _____   _____ + _____ = _____

_____ + _____ = _____   _____ + _____ = _____

_____ + _____ = _____   _____ + _____ = _____

Just the facts - Subtraction

_____ – _____ = _____   _____ – _____ = _____

_____ – _____ = _____   _____ – _____ = _____

_____ – _____ = _____   _____ – _____ = _____

_____ – _____ = _____   _____ – _____ = _____

_____ – _____ = _____   _____ – _____ = _____

_____ – _____ = _____   _____ – _____ = _____

_____ – _____ = _____   _____ – _____ = _____

_____ – _____ = _____   _____ – _____ = _____

(Directions are found on page 45.)

Picture the Problem

What is the problem? ______________________________

____

What do you know?

What do you need to find out?

Can you draw a picture of the problem?

Write your answer. ______________________________

____

Tips for Using Science Graphic Organizers

Graphic organizers are crucial for science. Students need reminders of different science concepts and processes in order to retain the information. Use these organizers both to help students become familiar with science curriculum elements such as life cycles and the scientific process, as well as to confirm their understanding of these elements.

Take a Closer Look
A magnifying glass is a perfect elementary science tool, and it also adds fun to the Take a Closer Look organizer (page 55). Help students sharpen their observation skills by having them look through a magnifier and then having them draw exactly what they see inside the lens. Ask students to label their drawings. You can also ask students to draw what they imagine that very tiny things, like germs, look like, or have them illustrate what they see through a microscope. (Cover the handle before copying and you have a round frame.)

Good Senses
The Use Good Senses organizer (page 56) helps students focus on making observations one sense at a time. Part of scientific inquiry is observation, and it is easy to forget that touch, smell, hearing, and taste (when appropriate) can be as informative as sight. (It is easy to cover or cut off taste at the bottom if it is not an appropriate sense for an activity.) Use the organizer when you want students to focus on each sense separately. Encourage students to draw representations of their observations as well as write about them.

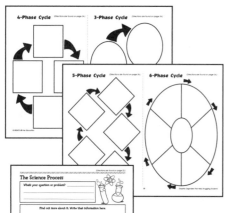

Cycle Organizers
Most elementary students are required to learn about cycles: plants, ladybugs, guppies, frogs, butterflies, and water, just to name a few. The Cycle organizers (pages 57 and 58) give you great flexibility when teaching about any of these or other cycles. Simply choose the cycle with the number of arrows that suits your purposes, fill in the type of cycle you wish to teach, and copy for students. Don't forget other cycles you could teach on the elementary level, such as recycling, deforestation and replanting, and even economic growth and decline. (For example, think about things like holiday spending and employment for this one.)

The Science Process
The Science Process organizer (page 59) is a quick overview of the scientific process with spaces for students to fill in information about experiments. Using this organizer, they can formulate their questions and hypotheses and decide what kind of experiments they should conduct. This also takes care of the preplanning so they can work on the experiment details.

The Experiment Planner
The Experiment Planner (page 60) helps students plan each step of an experiment. It is usually a good idea to let a student fill out the Planner and then review it with him so that you can help him add materials, insert additional steps (hence the space between steps), and fine-tune aspects of the experiment. After the review, let the students revise the experiment on a new Planner sheet. Let them write on additional sheets, if needed (but not on the back, so they can easily refer to their previous steps as they write new ones.)

(Directions are found on page 54.)

TAKE A CLOSER LOOK

Good Senses

3-Phase Cycle

(Directions are found on page 54.)

4-Phase Cycle

(Directions are found on page 54.)

6-Phase Cycle (Directions are found on page 54.)

5-Phase Cycle (Directions are found on page 54.)

(Directions are found on page 53.)

The Science Process

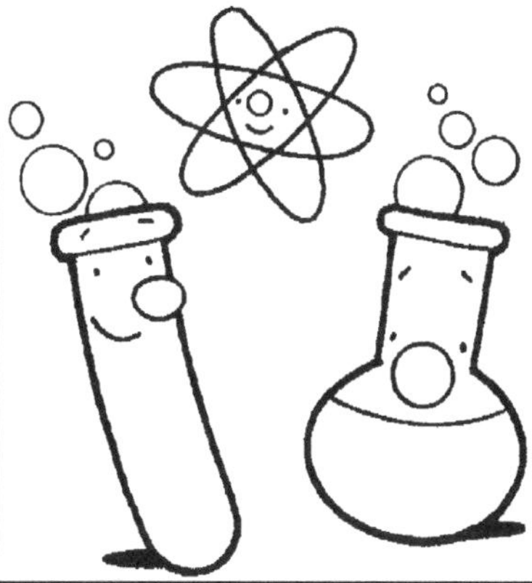

What's your question or problem? ______

______

______

Find out more about it. Write that information here.

______

______

______

______

______

What do you think the solution is?

______

______

______

______

How are you going to test it?

______

______

______

______

What were the test results?

______

______

______

______

 # The Experiment Planner

How are you going to test it?

_____

_____

_____

_____

What materials do you need?

- _____

- _____

- _____

- _____

Step 1.

_____

_____

_____

Step 2.

_____

_____

_____

Step 3.

_____

_____

_____

Step 4.

_____

_____

_____

Tips for Using Social Studies Graphic Organizers

Although many of the general organizers are effective for social studies experiences, here are some that especially apply themselves to the subject.

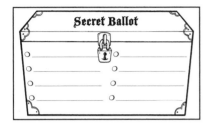

Secret Ballot

Use the Secret Ballot (below) to hold a mock election or to let students vote on any relevant topic, such as what type of cookies you will bring in for a class treat, what game to play at recess, where to go on a field trip, what silly celebration days to have during school spirit week, etc. If there are fewer items upon which to vote, cover the extra lines, or add more if needed. Be sure to discuss how a democracy operates as you let students cast their ballots. Count the votes as a classroom activity. If you want to let students write in suggestions, explain that they need to write them on the back of the secret ballot.

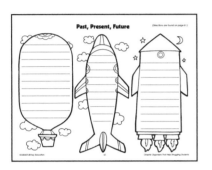

Past, Present, Future

The Past, Present, Future chart (page 62) can be used when talking about personal, local, national, or international history; technology; sociology; economics; or any other area of social studies. For example, let students chart the evolution of the telephone, the changes in available transportation, or the progress we have made in conserving energy. If you are near a building site, let them write and draw about the progress being made on the building, and discuss the positive and negative effects construction has. Have students bring in their parents' yearbooks and do past, present, and future charts of hairstyles or fashion. (Make sure you let students draw on poster board for this one!)

(Directions are found on page 61.)

Past, Present, Future

62

Correlations to the Standards

Graphic Organizers That Help Struggling Students supports the NCTE/IRA Standards for the English Language Arts, the recommended teaching practices outlined in the NAEYC/IRA position statement Learning to Read and Write: Developmentally Appropriate Practices for Young Children, the NCTM Principles and Standards for School Mathematics, the National Science Education Standards, and the Curriculum Standards for Social Studies.

NCTE/IRA Standards for the English Language Arts

The activities in this book support the following standards:

1. **Students read many different types of print and nonprint texts for a variety of purposes.** To use the graphic organizers in this book, students read both words and pictures.

2. **Students use a variety of strategies to build meaning while reading.** The graphic organizers in this book support such reading strategies and skills as following directions, predicting, sequencing, vocabulary development, and summarizing.

3. **Students communicate in spoken, written, and visual form, for a variety of purposes and a variety of audiences.** While completing the graphic organizers in this book, students communicate in drawing and in writing.

4. **Students use the writing process to write for different purposes and different audiences.** The "Reading and Writing Organizers" section of this book has several graphic organizers that focus specifically on the writing process.

5. **Students conduct research on a variety of topics and present their research findings in ways appropriate to their purpose and audience.** Several of the organizers in this book provide students with different ways to present their research in a variety of academic areas.

6. **Students use spoken, written, and visual language for their own purposes, such as to learn, for enjoyment, or to share information.** With graphic organizers, students use written and visual language to learn and to share information with others.

NAEYC/IRA Position Statement Learning to Read and Write: Developmentally Appropriate Practices for Young Children

The activities in this book support the following recommended teaching practices for Kindergarten and Primary students:

1. **Teachers read to children daily and provide opportunities for students to independently read both fiction and nonfiction texts.** Students use many of the graphic organizers in this book in conjunction with texts they have read.

2. **Teachers provide opportunities for students to write many different kinds of texts for different purposes.** Students write texts ranging from individual words to complete compositions while filling in the graphic organizers in this book.

3. **Teachers provide challenging instruction that expands children's knowledge of their world and expands vocabulary.** Many of the graphic organizers in this book help expand vocabulary.

4. **Teachers adapt teaching strategies based on the individual needs of a child.** The graphic organizers in this book have special features, such as large print, heavy cut lines, and parts that can be covered and omitted, that allow teachers to adapt the organizers to individual children's needs.

NCTM Principles and Standards for School Mathematics

This product and the activities in it support the following Number and Operations Standard Expectations for Grades Pre-K–2:

1. **Students count and recognize the number of objects in a set.** Several of the organizers in the math section of this book reinforce counting.

2. **Students understand the relative position and size of ordinal and cardinal numbers.** The Number Line organizer supports this standard.

3. **Students develop whole number sense and use numbers in flexible ways, including relating, composing, and decomposing them.** The House of Facts and Just the Facts organizers support this standard by presenting fact families.

4. **Students understand the meanings of addition and subtraction of whole numbers and how the two operations relate to each other.** The House of Facts and Just the Facts organizers support this standard by presenting fact families.

---

5. **Students use a variety of strategies for whole-number computation, focusing on addition and subtraction.** The House of Facts and Just the Facts organizers support this standard by presenting fact families.

6. **Students become fluent in basic number combinations for addition and subtraction.** The House of Facts and Just the Facts organizers support this standard.

This product and the activities in it support the following Algebra Standard Expectations for Grades Pre-K–2:
1. **Students sort, classify, and order objects by a variety of properties.** The Sorting Buckets, Timeline, Beginning, Middle, and End, and Venn Diagram graphic organizers support this standard.

This product and the activities in it support the following Geometry Standard Expectations for Grades Pre-K–2:
1. **Students identify, create, draw, compare, and sort two- and three-dimensional shapes.** The Geoboard Organizer supports this standard.

This product and the activities in it support the following Measurement Standard Expectations for Grades Pre-K–2:
1. **Students recognize the characteristics of length, volume, weight, area, and time.** The Calendar Grid and Daily Schedule organizers and the Measure Minder organizer support this standard.

2. **Students compare and order objects according to length, volume, weight, area, and/or time.** The Calendar Grid and Daily Schedule organizers and the Timeline organizer support this standard.

3. **Students select appropriate units and tools for the thing they are measuring.** The Measure Minder organizer supports this standard.

This product and the activities in it support the following Data Analysis and Probability Standard Expectations for Grades Pre-K–2:
1. **Students can ask questions and collect data about themselves and their worlds.** Since graphic organizers are used to collect and organize information, many of the organizers in this book support this standard.

2. **Students can sort and group objects according to their characteristics and organize information about the objects.** The Sorting Bucket and Venn Diagram organizers support this standard.

3. **Students can show data using objects, pictures, and graphs.** Many of the graphic organizers in this book support this standard, especially the Horizontal and Vertical Graph organizers.

National Science Education Standards

This book and the activities in it support the following Science as Inquiry standards for grades K–4:
1. **All students should develop the ability to do scientific inquiry.** The organizers in the science section of this book support this standard.

2. **All students should develop understanding of what scientific inquiry is.** The Good Senses organizer, The Science Process organizer, and The Experiment Planner organizer support this standard.

This book and the activities in it support the following Physical Science standards for grades K–4:
1. **All students should understand the properties of objects and materials.** The Good Senses organizer supports this standard.

This book and the activities in it support the following Life Science standards for grades K–4:
1. **All students should understand the life cycles of organisms.** The Cycle organizers support this standard.

National Council for the Social Studies Curriculum Standards for Social Studies

The activities in this book support the following performance expectations for students in the early grades:
1. **Students can correctly use time vocabulary such as past, present, future, and long ago; read and create simple timelines; identify examples of change; and recognize cause and effect relationships.** The Timeline, Beginning, Middle, End, and Past, Present, Future organizers support this standard.

2. **Students can use various sources, such as documents, maps, textbooks, and photographs to learn about the past.** The Past, Present, Future organizer supports this standard.

3. **Students can identify examples of the rights and responsibilities of citizens.** The Secret Ballot organizer supports this standard.